VOCAL SKIN

MOISTURIZING FACE CREAM

Nothing feels better than
wonderfully-hydrated soft skin, and
it starts with a routine.

VOCALSKINCARE.COM

Editor's Note

Dear Readers,

Welcome to this special issue of VMH Magazine, where we explore the concept of nourishing your inner light and embracing self-care. In a world that often feels overwhelming, it is crucial to take a step back and focus on nurturing our own well-being. This issue is dedicated to empowering you to prioritize self-care, embrace your inner richness, and achieve holistic success.

Self-care is a deeply personalized practice, unique to each individual. It encompasses taking care of our minds, bodies, and spirits. In this edition, we share inspiring stories that highlight the transformative power of self-care. These stories serve as reminders that prioritizing self-love and nurturing our inner light can lead to exceptional achievements in both our personal and professional lives.

We also explore key insights on teaching children healthy relationships. It is important to lay a strong foundation for healthy connections at an early age, as they shape our children's future. We provide strategies and resources to help children develop the necessary skills to foster loving and respectful relationships, building a brighter future for generations to come.

Moreover, we invite you to embark on soul-enriching adventures through solo travel. Exploring new places and immersing ourselves in different cultures can inspire personal growth and self-discovery. We share stories of individuals who embarked on transformative solo journeys, unlocking new dimensions of self-awareness and expanding their horizons.

On a global scale, we present an exclusive feature on the Global Trade & Supply Summit held in the beautiful city of Dubai, UAE. This summit brought together leaders and experts from various industries to discuss global trade and its impact on economic growth and stability. We delve into the opportunities and challenges presented by the rapidly changing global trade landscape, shedding light on how it affects businesses and economies worldwide.

Lastly, we turn our attention to The White House Initiative for HBCUs (Historically Black Colleges and Universities) in America. This initiative aims to enhance the educational experiences and opportunities for students attending HBCUs. We highlight the impact of this initiative and share success stories of individuals who have benefited from the support and resources provided by HBCUs.

At VMH Magazine, we firmly believe that self-care should be an integral part of our lives, rather than a fleeting luxury. It is vital to invest time and effort in our own well-being to maintain balance in all aspects of life. We encourage you to reflect on your own self-care strategies and explore new ways to cultivate your inner richness.

While reading through this issue, we hope you feel inspired to prioritize self-care and ignite your inner light. Remember, self-care is not selfish; it is a necessary foundation for personal growth, happiness, and success. So, take a moment, breathe deeply, and immerse yourself in the wisdom shared within these pages. May they kindle the flame that nourishes your inner light and guide you on a path to true fulfillment.

Vikki Jones

Editor-in-Chief

Table of Contents

Cover Image: Vikki Jones
Photography Credit: Vikki Jones

THE BIDEN-HARRIS ADMINISTRATION'S COMMITMENT TO SUPPORTING HISTORICALLY BLACK COLLEGES AND UNIVERSITIES

President Joe Biden reaffirmed his commitment to historically Black colleges and universities (HBCUs) and their vital role in promoting educational equity, excellence, and opportunity. This commitment was further showcased at the annual National HBCU Week Conference, where various stakeholders gathered to discuss strategies for advancing education and strengthening the role of HBCUs. The Biden-Harris Administration's historic actions and investments in HBCUs are a testament to their recognition of these institutions' value and their vision for a more inclusive higher education system.

The achievements of HBCU graduates are admirable and speak to the impact of these institutions. HBCUs, which represent only 3% of colleges and universities, have produced a significant number of Black engineers, teachers, doctors, dentists, judges, and even the first woman and Black and South Asian Vice President of the United States. These achievements highlight the importance of HBCUs in promoting economic mobility within the African American community.

For over 180 years, HBCUs have been at the forefront of promoting equity, access, and excellence in education. The Biden-Harris Administration has recognized their pivotal role and has made historic investments totaling over $7 billion to support HBCUs. These investments include funding through the American Rescue Plan and other COVID relief measures, capital finance debt relief for public and private HBCUs, grant funding to expand academic capacity, and support for low-income students.

Moreover, the 2022 and 2023 spending packages have further demonstrated the Administration's commitment to supporting HBCUs. This includes providing flexibilities for minority-serving institutions to use funds for infrastructure needs related to the pandemic, increasing Pell Grants by $900 to ease financial burdens on HBCU students, establishing a grant program for research and development infrastructure, and investing in HBCU institutional development and diversification of the teaching profession.

The Biden-Harris Administration has also drawn attention to funding inequities for 1890 land-grant institutions. Secretaries Miguel Cardona and Thomas Vilsack addressed the significant funding disparity between HBCUs and their non-HBCU land-grant peers, which has hindered HBCUs' access to resources and infrastructure development.

This emphasis on equitable funding underscores the importance of ensuring HBCUs can fulfill their potential in driving innovation and empowering talented and diverse students and communities. Additionally, the U.S. Department of Education has played a crucial role in supporting HBCUs facing violence. By securing Project SERV funds, over $2.4 million has been allocated to HBCUs affected by bomb threats, enabling them to restore safe learning environments and invest in students' mental health.

Furthermore, the Department of Education has collaborated with other government agencies to pioneer new programs in support of HBCUs. These initiatives include the U.S. Air Force's first-ever HBCU-led University Affiliated Research Center, the Department of Commerce's Connecting-Minority-Communities program, the Department of Transportation's University Transportation Center led by Prairie View A&M University, and the Department of Energy's Funding for Accelerated, Inclusive Research Program. These

programs aim to enhance research capacity, infrastructure, and expertise at historically excluded institutions.

The National Science Foundation has also introduced initiatives to break down barriers in STEM fields that disproportionately affect minority-serving institutions. These efforts include the GRANTED program, which encourages transformative ideas and scalable models, and NASA's investment in HBCUs to support programs in artificial intelligence and machine learning.

The Biden-Harris Administration's commitment to HBCUs is commendable and reflects its dedication to promoting educational equity, excellence, and opportunity. The investments, initiatives, and support provided will foster the continued growth and success of HBCUs, empowering generations of talented individuals and creating a more inclusive and valuable higher education system.

As President Biden stated, "The future is bright for HBCUs." It is our collective responsibility to ensure that these institutions, which have played a vital role in shaping our nation's history, have the resources and support they need to continue making a positive impact on students and communities for generations to come.

5 Tips to Improve Small Business Productivity

FAMILY FEATURES

Businesses that run efficiently often find continued, long-term success. However, running a small business comes with a multitude of challenges that can hinder productivity.

Between hiring employees, managing payroll, handling customer relations, delivering products, meeting with staff and other tasks, it's important to take steps to help your business work smarter, not harder, while maintaining productivity. More efficient workdays mean more projects or tasks can be completed, giving you an advantage in a competitive marketplace.

To help improve productivity and create a more efficient work environment, consider these tips from the experts at Pitney Bowes, a global shipping and mailing company that has worked for more than 100 years to provide technology, logistics, financial services and solutions that help enterprises thrive and small business owners operate right from their homes including the PitneyShip Cube, which simplifies shipping packages and e-commerce orders while saving time and space.

Set Goals

Setting goals for your operation is vital to building a productive business and ensuring your employees understand your vision and how they can actively contribute to the company's success. Whether you're a startup or an established business with multiple employees, set realistic, well-defined goals that are in line with your business strategy, like investing in office tools and solutions that can help you discover efficiencies. Periodically revisit those goals to ensure you're on track to meet them and make any adjustments as necessary. For example, working from home may provide an opportunity to save on rent and enable you to allocate those savings toward upgraded office equipment.

Delegate Less Critical Responsibilities

Remember, you can't do it all by yourself. In the same way it's important to prioritize your list of tasks, delegation is key to improving productivity. Passing on some of the work, such as designing email templates, writing blog posts, creating white papers and more, to your employees allows you to maximize your limited time. Think through additional ways for others to lessen the load, like using a cloud-based shipping solution to streamline the process and ensure alignment in task sharing. Even if you're a solo entrepreneur, look at what tasks you may be able to outsource to a third-party vendor to free up some of your time.

Simplify Shipping

If your business sells a product, shipping may be a time-consuming, expensive part of your operation. Leave the post office behind and save valuable time with an option like the PitneyShip Cube, an all-in-one, Wi-Fi-enabled thermal shipping label printer with a built-in scale. It includes companion software and can integrate with your current online store to automatically import order details then easily print the shipping labels and postage. You can weigh packages, compare discounted shipping rates and automatically share tracking notifications via email.

"One of the biggest barriers for small businesses are shipping costs," said Shemin Nurmohamed, president, sending technology solutions, Pitney Bowes. "Our goal is to allow clients to take advantage of what larger shippers get in terms of discounts while saving them the critical time they need to work on their core businesses. With the PitneyShip Cube, the first shipping label printer of its kind with a built-in scale and companion software, users are able to ship faster and smarter. This product is ideal for both e-commerce and office shippers looking to save time and space by streamlining their processes and eliminating unnecessary equipment. Plus, it can save users money as it provides a discount of 3 cents on First Class stamps, up to 89% on USPS Priority Mail and up to 82% off UPS standard rates."

By completing all the necessary tasks beforehand, you'll skip the post office line and allow yourself to focus on more profitable endeavors. You can also track parcels throughout their shipping journey with data that can be shared with customers for a smooth shipping experience.

Streamline Software

A quick and easy way to increase productivity and efficiency is taking advantage of technology like software as a service platforms. Particularly true in this age of hybrid and remote workers, cloud-based communications software can keep your team members on the same page, regardless of their location, to help your company keep up with important information such as ever-changing carrier rates to quickly identify the best shipping and fulfillment options. With available platforms that combine team messaging, video conferencing, task management, file sharing and storage, it can be simple to stay connected with your employees. Additional cloud-based software for everything from payroll to word processing and graphic design is also readily available to help further streamline your business's technology. Knowledge is power and combining all this information in one place can give you greater control over your organization as a whole.

Learn from Your Customers

When looking for ways to improve, start by asking your customers for honest feedback. Creating customer satisfaction surveys provides you with a fresh perspective while giving customers a voice so they can feel valued. Plus, it can help you build a rapport with customers as they know their voices are heard while you discover what's working, what isn't and ways you can improve the business.

Find more solutions for improving your productivity and efficiency in the workplace at pitneybowes.com.

Visit PitneyBowes.com

TRVL BAGS

@shopvikkijones

DESIGNS BY
VIKKI JONES

The Power of Transformation & Facets of the Heart
Dontisha James

Dontisha James' book "Facets of the Heart" offers a powerful testimony to the transformative power of spirituality and how it can heal and guide individuals towards finding their purpose and true selves. By recognizing the connection between childbirth and spiritual rebirth, understanding the importance of a deep relationship with God, and relying on His grace, James' shows that it is possible to overcome pain, rejection, and struggles. Transforming our hearts allows us to experience the true joy, peace, and love that come from living in alignment with God's purpose for our lives.

Overcoming Pain, Rejection, and Struggles: A Guide to Transforming Your Heart

Transforming our hearts requires us to go through deep introspection, reflection, and an understanding of our emotions and past experiences. Dontisha James' personal journey of trauma, pain, grief, depression, and anxiety is a guide and testimony for readers who are struggling with similar experiences. By acknowledging and dealing with our past struggles, we can transform our hearts and become happier, more fulfilled individuals with alignment to God's plan for us.

Dontisha James' book highlights a unique connection between childbirth and spiritual rebirth. She believes that life-changing moments such as childbirth can open a spiritual gateway that allows individuals to experience a transformative power that awakens their spiritual senses. This approach helps readers to understand the importance of spiritual rebirth in their lives and guides them to realize its potential in healing and transforming their hearts.

Living in Alignment with God's Purpose – Experiencing True Joy, Peace, and Love

Transforming our hearts requires us to develop a deep relationship with God and follow His purpose for our lives. Dontisha James's book provides essential tools to guide readers on their spiritual journey to live a life in alignment with God's purpose. Through this journey, readers learn to experience true joy, peace, and love that comes with living a life of purpose and alignment with God's will.In conclusion, Dontisha James' book "Facets of the Heart" is a life-changing guide for individuals who want to transform their hearts, overcome pain, suffering, and find alignment with God's purpose for their lives. By recognizing the connection between childbirth and spiritual rebirth, understanding the importance of a deep relationship with God, and relying on His grace, readers can transform their lives and live joyously, peacefully, and in alignment with their divine calling.

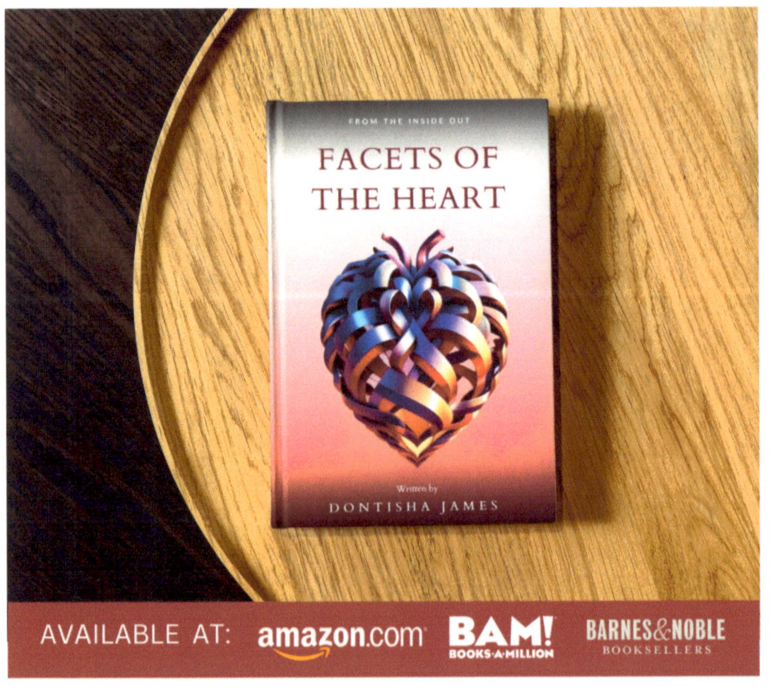

NAVIGATING THE AI REVOLUTION: 4 ESSENTIAL TIPS FOR NEXT-LEVEL BUSINESS SUCCESS

In the age of AI, businesses need to adapt and evolve to stay competitive. This article explores four essential tips that can help businesses thrive in the era of artificial intelligence. The tips include embracing AI technology to enhance productivity and efficiency, investing in AI talent and expertise, leveraging data for insights and personalization, and prioritizing data privacy and ethics. By implementing these strategies, businesses can unlock new opportunities, deliver exceptional customer experiences, and drive growth in the rapidly evolving landscape of AI.

Embrace AI Technology

To stay ahead in the age of AI, businesses should embrace and integrate AI technology into their operations. By leveraging AI, businesses can enhance productivity, efficiency, and customer experience.

Invest in AI Talent and Expertise

To successfully implement AI strategies, businesses need to invest in acquiring AI talent and expertise. Additionally, businesses should provide continuous training and upskilling opportunities to their employees to ensure they can effectively work with AI technology.

Leverage Data for Insights

Data is a valuable asset. Businesses can collect, analyze, and leverage data to gain insights into customer preferences, and market trends. By utilizing AI algorithms, businesses can identify patterns, and deliver personalized experiences at scale.

Prioritize Data Privacy and Ethics

As AI becomes more prevalent, businesses must prioritize data privacy and ethics. Additionally, businesses should establish ethical guidelines for AI usage. By prioritizing data privacy and ethics, businesses can build trust with their customers and stakeholders.

www.vmhmagazine.com | advertising@vmhmagazine.com

Embrace Your Potential and Achieve Extraordinary Success

Written by Vikki Jones

In a world filled with immense possibilities and endless opportunities, it is disheartening to witness countless individuals holding themselves back from realizing their full potential. Far too often, self-doubt and fear of failure prevent us from taking that leap of faith and embracing our greatness. But what if, just for a moment, we set aside our doubts and allowed ourselves to truly explore our strengths, talents, and unique abilities? What if we dared to think outside of the box and invested in our belief in ourselves? The results could be nothing short of extraordinary.

Each one of us possesses an incredible reservoir of untapped potential. However, it is only by giving ourselves a chance that we can unlock this hidden greatness. It begins with a journey inward, a sincere examination of our strengths and talents. By identifying and developing these strong points, we lay the foundation for our success.

Think of yourself as a diamond in the rough. You have the potential to shine brilliantly, but it requires effort, patience, and a willingness to invest in self-improvement. Take the time to discover what truly brings you joy and fulfillment. Nurture those passions and talents, for they are the keys to unlocking your greatness.

It is also crucial to break free from the confines of conventional thinking. The world is changing rapidly, and the most successful individuals are those who can adapt and think outside of the box.

Embrace innovation, challenge the status quo, and be unafraid to take calculated risks. By doing so, you open up a world of possibilities and pave the way for greatness to flow into your life.

However, none of this is possible without a strong belief in oneself. Confidence is the driving force behind every successful person. Believe in your abilities, your dreams, and your potential. Surround yourself with positive influences, seek out mentors who can guide you, and never underestimate the power of self-affirmation.

It is important to recognize that greatness does not come easily or overnight. It is a journey, filled with obstacles and setbacks. But it is through these challenges that we grow, learn, and become stronger. Embrace failure as a stepping stone to success and never let setbacks deter you from pursuing your dreams.

So, dear reader, I implore you to give yourself a chance. Look deep within, develop your strong points, and allow yourself the opportunity to think outside of the box. Invest in and strengthen your belief in yourself. Know that you have what it takes to be great. Believe it, embrace it, and watch as your greatness flows effortlessly into every aspect of your life.

EXCLUSIVE

ELEVATION
STRATEGIES

TAKE YOUR BUSINESS
TO NEW HEIGHTS

VIKKIMJONES.COM

LAKEISHA DIXON JONES

Written by Vikki Jones

TRANSFORMING PASSION INTO
SWEET SUCCESS

From Childhood Memories to Baking Success: The Inspiring Journey of the Savory & Sweet Treats Founder

"Both of my grandmothers were avid bakers, and some of my most cherished childhood memories are intertwined with the aroma of freshly baked buttermilk biscuits and sizzling bacon, accompanied by the soulful sounds of gospel music filling the Sunday morning air," reminisces Lakeisha Dixon Jones, the owner and founder of Savory & Sweet Treats. She fondly recalls the love and warmth that permeated her early years, as her grandmothers Sarah Smith and Estell Dixon created delectable delights in their kitchens.

Lakeisha's paternal grandmother, in particular, played a significant role in nurturing her love for baking. Summoning her into the kitchen, she would share the joy of licking the spoon clean after mixing cake batter. These simple moments became the foundation of Lakeisha's deep love for the art of baking, firmly rooted in the warmth and nostalgia of her childhood.

Unfortunately, tragedy struck, and both of Lakeisha's beloved grandmothers passed away before she reached the age of ten. They didn't leave behind a cookbook of recipes, but they gifted her something far more valuable —memories that would fuel her lifelong passion for baking.

Driven by these cherished memories, Lakeisha dedicated herself to honing her baking skills, experimenting with flavors, and developing her own unique recipes. As she grew older, she also found herself drawn to the field of coaching, specializing in both life and business coaching.

"For over a decade, I've been dedicated to the field of coaching, specializing in both life and business coaching," Lakeisha shares. "There's an incredible satisfaction in helping individuals build themselves up and strategize for success. Combining my passion for coaching with my love for baking, I decided to venture into a unique business—teaching techniques and business strategies within the world of baking. It came naturally to me because I find immense joy in both coaching and baking. These seemingly distinct industries share a common thread: the power of coaching to guide individuals through their passions, challenges, and obstacles. Coaching, I've discovered, is a universal tool that transcends industries."

And so, Savory & Sweet Treats was born, offering a fusion of coaching and baking expertise. What truly sets Lakeisha apart as a baking coach is her distinctive personality and coaching style. Her ability to connect with fellow bakers on a deeper level allows her to impart not only the technical skills necessary for baking pound cakes but also a sense of creativity and innovation.

"My unique approach helps bakers create not just delectable treats but also a sustainable cash flow in their businesses," Lakeisha explains. "Through coaching, I empower individuals to turn their passions into successful ventures, guiding them in identifying market demands, developing business strategies, and instilling an entrepreneurial mindset. I believe that baking is an art form, and I'm committed to nurturing the talents and dreams of aspiring bakers."

Lakeisha's journey from childhood memories to baking success is an inspiring testament to the power of passion, determination, and the influence of loved ones. Her grandmothers' presence in the kitchen shaped her love for baking, while her coaching skills propelled her to transform her passion into a thriving business.

In sharing her story and teaching others, Lakeisha offers a guiding light for those who aspire to follow their passions. She reminds us all that cherished memories and the guidance of loved ones can pave the way for a successful and fulfilling journey.

DUBAI + THE ECONOMIST GLOBAL TRADE & SUPPLY CHAIN SUMMIT HIGHLIGHTS

By VIKKI JONES

Held in Dubai, a future-forward city, the event captured the spirit of innovation and collaboration necessary for navigating the complexities of the modern trade landscape.

The Economist Impact's Global Trade and Supply Chain Summit has become a vital platform for business leaders, policymakers, and thought leaders to come together and discuss the ever-changing landscape of trade policy and practical business logistics. With its third edition held in the vibrant city of Dubai, the summit provided valuable insights into topics such as supply chain diversification, sustainability, product traceability, digital trade, supply chain resilience, and emerging regions. Prominent speakers, including H.E. Mohammad Ali bin Rashed Lootah, President and CEO of Dubai Chambers, emphasized the importance of the voice of the business community in shaping trade policies. and thought leaders to come together and discuss the ever-changing landscape of trade policy and practical business logistics. With its third edition held in the vibrant city of Dubai, the summit provided valuable insights into topics such as supply chain diversification, sustainability, product

traceability, digital trade, supply chain resilience, and emerging regions. Prominent speakers, including H.E. Mohammad Ali bin Rashed Lootah, President and CEO of Dubai Chambers, emphasized the importance of the voice of the business community in shaping trade policies.

UAE's Role in Transforming Trade:

Another notable speaker was H.E. Dr. Thani bin Ahmed Al Zeyoudi, UAE Minister of State for Foreign Trade. Dr. Al Zeyoudi spoke about the UAE's ambition to become a central location in the global value chain by redefining supply chains and forging new partnerships. With a focus on securing Comprehensive Economic Partnerships and Agreements with strategic allies worldwide, the UAE aims to boost exports by at least 50 percent by 2030. In the face of decoupling and uncertainty, the UAE is actively transforming trade to fuel growth and investment.

H.E. Mohammad Ali bin Rashed Lootah, President and CEO of Dubai Chambers

Photo Credit: Vikki Jones

H.E. Thani bin Ahmed Al Zeyoudi Minister of state for foreign trade, UAE

Photo Credit: Garry Jones

Building Resilience in Supply Chain Operations:

Mahmoud Aboueldahab, Head of Supply Chain - Middle East at Imdad, shed light on building resilience in supply chain operations. Aboueldahab stressed the need for businesses to assess the quality management systems and products of their suppliers, emphasizing respect and trust as essential factors. He highlighted the significance of evaluating the financial situation and safety measures of suppliers, considering the overall ecosystem.

Aboueldahab also outlined several crucial tasks that businesses involved in

> In the context of trade and supply chains, digital transformation offers immense opportunities for efficiency, transparency, and improved customer experiences.

supply chain operations should incorporate into their checklists. Continuous collaboration, active engagement, and supply development programs were emphasized as important elements for ensuring integration with suppliers.

Digital Transformation Landscape: Unlocking Opportunities and Addressing Challenges

Digital transformation in trade and supply chains has emerged as a significant topic of discussion at the Economist Impact's Global Trade and Supply Chain Summit. The summit brought together experts to explore the opportunities and challenges that technology presents for industries to grow and thrive in a digital age.

Technology has already demonstrated its potential in various sectors, from banking to book selling. In the context of trade and supply chains, digital transformation offers immense opportunities for efficiency, transparency, and improved customer experiences. However, it also introduces new challenges that businesses must address to fully leverage its benefits.

Prioritizing Compliance in the Competitive Market

A panel focused on the importance of trade compliance for businesses, especially with the increasing number of trade rules and regulations. Mohamed Eldabaa emphasized the need for companies to have a good product, as well as complying with various regulations, to ensure success in the market. This sentiment was echoed by the other panelists, emphasizing the need for businesses to not only comply with trade regulations but also stay informed and up-to-date on evolving trade policies.

The Economist Impact's Global Trade and Supply Chain Summit proved to be an informative and forward-thinking event, offering valuable insights and perspectives for businesses of all sizes. The summit showcased the significance of engaging the business community in trade policy discussions and emphasized the importance of building resilient supply chains through collaboration, respect, and active involvement of suppliers.

Discover Atlanta's Hidden Gems!

LOOKING FOR THE HOTTEST NEW SPOTS IN ATLANTA? LOOK NO FURTHER THAN **NEW SPOT ALERT ATL**!

WE PERSONALLY VISIT AND VET EACH LOCATION TO BRING YOU THE BEST OF:

Dining: From upscale to casual eateries, we've got you covered!

Entertainment: Explore exciting venues for a night out on the town!

Beauty: Find businesses to enhance your beauty and self-care routines!

Join our Instagram community @newspotalertatl and let us guide you through Atlanta's culinary and entertainment scene. Trust our recommendations - we've got the inside scoop!

Don't miss out on the newest and best spots in Atlanta!

FOLLOW US

TikTok: @newspotalertatl

Instagram:@newspotalertatl

UNLOCK YOUR LITERARY POTENTIAL WITH VMH PUBLISHING

At VMH Publishing, we stand as a beacon of intellectual excellence, fueling the literary world with our unwavering commitment to literary brilliance. As a distinguished publishing house, we are dedicated to unearthing the limitless potential of language and ushering in a new era of profound literary works.

Whether you're a reader seeking an enthralling narrative, an aspiring author yearning to be discovered, or a literary enthusiast eager to explore new horizons, VMH Publishing invites you to embark on a journey of literary discovery. Immerse yourself in thought-provoking stories, poetic prose, and insightful non-fiction that will leave an indelible mark on your mind and heart.

Visit our website, www.vmhpublishing.net, to explore our captivating catalog and join us in our mission to celebrate the power of words. Together, let's redefine literary excellence and shape the future of literature.

WWW.VMHPUBLISHING.NET
NEW YORK, NY 10007

NURTURING YOUR INNER LIGHT

Prioritizing Self-Care and Well-Being

BY VIKKI JONES

In the bustle of today's world, it is imperative to prioritize your well-being and mental health. As human beings, we often find ourselves in toxic environments or surrounded by unhealthy relationships that drain our energy and impact our overall sense of self. This article delves into the importance of self-care, mindfulness, and the recognition of warning signs that prompt us to take action to protect ourselves. By choosing to distance ourselves from negativity and embracing healthy, fulfilling practices, we can nourish our souls and experience the joys that life has to offer.

Taking Heed of Warning Signs:

One of the crucial steps to safeguarding our well-being is to pay attention to warning signs that can alert us to toxic individuals or situations. Whether it be in friendships, professional relationships, or even marriages, recognizing and understanding the characteristics and personalities of others can help us identify when we need to take action.

When you notice your inner light beginning to dim, it is essential to take immediate action. Seek out ways to distance yourself from the negativity that is impacting your well-being. Remember, you always have a choice, and there is always something you can do to protect yourself.

Knowing and Nurturing Yourself:

In the quest for self-care, it is fundamental to prioritize self-awareness. You are the expert on yourself, and if you have yet to fully understand who you are, it is time to embark on that journey of self-discovery. Take the time for self-reflection and dig deep into understanding your needs, desires, and what truly brings you joy from within.

In a world that often emphasizes sticking with things, jobs, or relationships that may be harming us, it is crucial to break free from societal expectations and prioritize our own well-being. Learning to nourish our souls in healthy, fulfilling ways allows us to create a space that promotes growth, positivity, and genuine happiness.

Digital Detox and Self-Reflection:

In an era dominated by technology, it is essential to be mindful of the impact it can have on our mental health. Engaging in a digital detox can provide an opportunity for self-reflection and realignment with our inner selves. Taking time away from screens allows us to recalibrate and focus on our well-being without the constant distractions and pressures of social media or digital communication.

Make Adjustments
for a Healthier Life

During this digital detox, make a conscious effort to reflect on your needs and wants. Ask yourself: What truly makes you feel good inside? What activities bring you joy and fulfillment? By identifying these aspects, you can intentionally prioritize them in your life, ensuring that you are continuously nurturing your own well-being.

Investing in Self-Love:

One powerful way to foster self-care and well-being is by investing in self-love and treating yourself with kindness and compassion. Take yourself out on a date and indulge in activities that bring you joy. This simple act of self-love can have a profound impact on your overall well-being and help you build a strong foundation of self-worth.

Remember, sometimes we cannot change our external environments or jobs, but we can always control how we nourish our souls. Surround yourself with friends who uplift you, bring laughter into your life, and cherish the person you are. Seek out those relationships that encourage growth, positivity, and support your journey towards self-discovery and fulfillment.

In a world full of negativity and toxic influences, prioritizing self-care and well-being is of utmost importance. By paying attention to warning signs, knowing and nurturing ourselves, engaging in digital detox, and investing in self-love, we can cultivate a vibrant, fulfilled life. Remember, you are the author of your own happiness, and taking care of yourself should be your number one priority. Embrace the power within you, protect your well-being, and experience the joys that life has to offer.

A Simple Self-Care Strategy for Everyday Well-being

By incorporating a simple self-care strategy into our daily routine, we can nurture ourselves, recharge our energies, and flourish both personally and professionally. Here's a practical and effective self-care strategy to help you navigate the challenges of everyday life:

1. Mindful Mornings:
Start your day with a few mindful moments dedicated to nurturing your mind, body, and spirit. Begin by setting intentions for the day, practicing deep breathing exercises, or engaging in a short meditation. Allow yourself time for a healthy breakfast and moments of gratitude, focusing on positive affirmations to set a positive tone for the day ahead.

2. Nourishing Movement:
Physical activity is not only crucial for our physical health but also for our mental and emotional well-being. Incorporate some form of movement into your daily routine, whether it's yoga, jogging, dancing, or a brisk walk in nature. Find an activity that brings you joy and makes you feel good from the inside out.

3. Digital Detox:
Set aside designated times throughout the day to disconnect from electronic devices, allowing yourself to unwind and engage in activities that bring you joy and relaxation. Rediscover the pleasure of reading a book, spending time in nature, pursuing a hobby, or simply engaging in mindful activities that don't require screens.

4. Healthy Eating Habits:
Fueling our bodies with nourishing foods plays a vital role in self-care. Prioritize a balanced diet, incorporating wholesome foods, and staying hydrated throughout the day. Practice mindful eating, savoring each bite and listening to your body's hunger and fullness cues.

5. Restorative Self-Care Practices:
Prioritize activities that bring you peace, relaxation, and joy. This could include indulging in a warm bubble bath, practicing aromatherapy, journaling, painting, or listening to soothing music. Engage in activities that calm your mind and replenish your soul.

Customize this strategy to suit your needs and make it an integral part of your daily routine. .

MADE TO LOVE
FOSTERING HEALTHY RELATIONSHIPS THROUGH AWARENESS

Written by Vikki Jones

EMPOWERING CHILDREN TO RECOGNIZE AND AVOID ABUSE IN RELATIONSHIPS

Abuse is a serious issue that can manifest in various forms within relationships. Whether it is between spouses, dating partners, or even friends, recognizing the signs of unhealthy dynamics is crucial. Developing this awareness early on is essential for fostering healthy friendships, relationships, and marriages. Vikki Jones, drawing from her own childhood experiences, understands the importance of steering clear from individuals who exhibit abusive behavior.

Jones's childhood served as a foundation for her understanding of what types of boys and men to avoid. This understanding has proven invaluable as she navigates through life, enabling her to identify and avoid individuals displaying abusive conduct. Abuse can take on many forms, such as verbal, mental, emotional, and physical, and Jones wants children, especially young girls, to recognize that they are Made To Love and deserve to be treated with respect.

To spread this message, Jones has written a children's book titled "Made To Love," which aims to raise awareness among girls and boys about appropriate conduct. The book's main character, Payton, learns the importance of staying away from unfriendly boys, while Justin, another character, receives a valuable lesson on managing his emotions when things don't go his way.

By teaching children about healthy behavior early on, Jones hopes to equip them with the tools to identify and avoid abusive relationships in the future.

Furthermore, in an effort to reinforce the message that everyone deserves love and respect, Jones has created a new toy doll. This doll serves as a reminder to all girls who hug or play with it that they are Made To Love. By incorporating this tangible reminder into playtime, Jones hopes to instill a sense of self-worth and encourage children to seek out healthy relationships and friendships.

Abuse should never be excused or tolerated in any form. Recognizing the signs of abuse and teaching children about healthy behavior from a young age is crucial for fostering positive relationships. Through her children's book and toy doll, Vikki Jones is actively working to bring awareness to the issue of abuse and empower children to recognize and avoid unhealthy dynamics. Every child deserves to know that they are Made To Love and should be treated with kindness and respect.

BOOK & DOLL

Payton Learns a Lesson on Boys & Behavior. In this story Payton learns what it means to recognize good and bad behavior in boys. After an incident on the playground, Payton's mom teaches her what to look for in nice friends. The little boy in the story - Justin - is taught by his parents, lessons on how to treat girls, and why.

MADE TO LOVE

What is
THE
SIMPLICITY OF
INDULGING
ONES PASSION

Ignite Passion for Your Work and Thrive

Passion Stimulates Value & Success If you have dreams, goals, and aspirational things you want to do with your life, go for it! Associate with people who will add to you and your goals versus take away from them. Get away from those folks that don't support your idea, and surround yourself with people that support and value you - help you grow.

@vmhmagazine

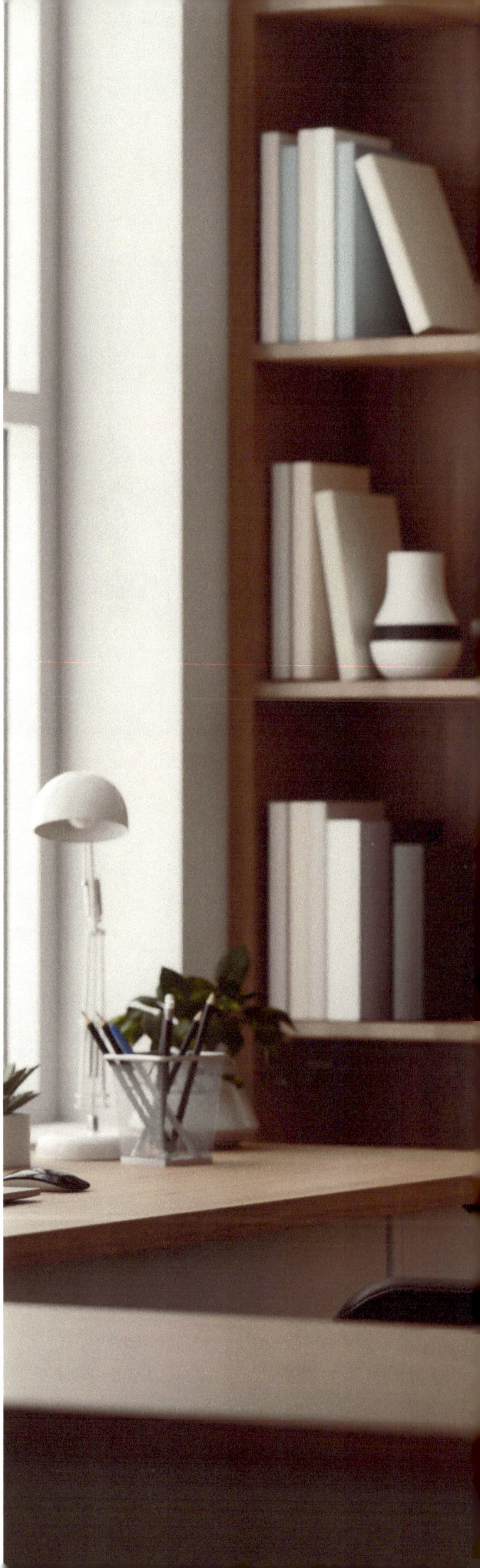

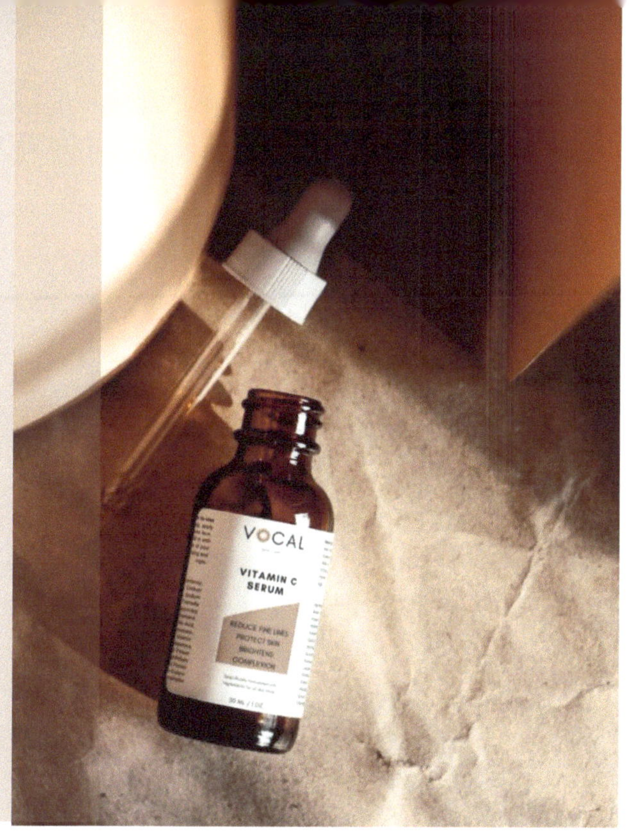

NOURISH
HYDRATE
YOUR SKIN

EXCELLENT
SKIN CARE
FOR ALL
SKIN
TONES!

More info: www.vocalskincare.com

Dr. Artesius Miller: Pioneering Education for Equity & Excellence - The Utopian Academy for the Arts Charter School

Dr. Artesius Miller, the Founder & CEO of the Utopian Academy for the Arts Charter School, is a visionary leader in K-12 education. His passion for creating better educational opportunities for Black and brown students led him to establish the first authorized charter school by the State Charter Schools Commission of Georgia.

Reflecting on the journey of Utopian Academy, Dr. Miller expresses his motivation and the driving force behind his work. He shares, "Going back to 2009, when I saw the fifth-largest school system in the state of Georgia lose accreditation, the second time in American history that this had happened. For a community comprised of Black and brown kids, I wanted something better. I wanted to reshape the narrative for what has historically been the outcomes for students in Clayton County, Georgia."

This commitment to challenging the status quo and providing a transformative educational experience for students has been at the forefront of Dr. Miller's decision-making process. He emphasizes the need to disrupt public education and offer innovative and creative solutions to students who have traditionally lacked access to such opportunities.

Dr. Miller firmly believes that complacency should never be the standard in education. He states, "The status quo had become just the norm, and we had to disrupt public education in a way that parents and students were looking for." By doing so, he aimed to ensure that students in Atlanta, Georgia, especially those residing on the economically disadvantaged South side, had equal access to quality education.

The Utopian Academy for the Arts Charter School Network, under Dr. Miller's leadership, has successfully provided a platform for students to explore and excel in the arts. By integrating arts education into the curriculum, Utopian Academy offers a holistic learning experience that nurtures creativity, critical thinking, and self-expression.

Utopian Academy for the Arts Charter School Network celebrates its 10-year anniversary, Dr. Miller reflects on the progress made and the impact created. He shares, "Throughout the years, my motivation has been to ensure that students who traditionally would not have had that level of access based upon the geography of where they live, have access and opportunities."

Timing for Success: Mastering the Art of Achieving Goals

Written by Vikki Jones

Timing is a critical element when it comes to achieving success and reaching our goals. Just like a well-choreographed dance, being in sync with the right moment can make all the difference. It's not just about working hard or having a solid plan; it's about understanding when to take action, when to pivot, and when to seize opportunities. Recognizing the importance of timing and mastering its art can significantly enhance our chances of success.

One key aspect of timing for success is knowing when to start. Oftentimes, we may find ourselves waiting for the perfect moment, waiting for all the stars to align. However, it's important to remember that waiting for the ideal conditions can lead to missed opportunities. Instead, we should focus on taking that initial step and starting towards our goals. As the saying goes, "The best time to plant a tree was 20 years ago. The second best time is now." By taking action and starting, we set ourselves on the path to success.

However, timing is not just about starting; it's also about recognizing when to make adjustments. As we progress towards our goals, we may encounter obstacles or unforeseen circumstances. Being able to adapt and adjust our strategies is crucial. Sometimes, it's about being patient and allowing things to unfold naturally. Other times, it's about making bold and timely decisions to steer ourselves back on track. The ability to assess the situation, gauge the right moment, and make necessary adjustments can be a game-changer in achieving our goals. Timing also plays a significant role in seizing opportunities. Opportunities often present themselves unexpectedly, and it's up to us to recognize them and act swiftly. This requires being alert, staying informed, and having a clear vision of our goals. By staying attuned to our surroundings and having a proactive mindset, we position ourselves to capitalize on these opportunities when they arise. As the saying goes, "Luck is what happens when preparation meets opportunity." By being prepared and having a keen sense of timing, we can create our own luck and open doors to success.

Furthermore, timing is closely tied to perseverance. Sometimes, success doesn't come overnight, and it requires patience and persistence. It's important to understand that

timing is not always within our control. There may be setbacks and delays along the way. However, by maintaining our focus, staying committed, and continuously working towards our goals, we position ourselves to be ready for the right moment when it arrives. Timing and perseverance go hand in hand, and together, they can propel us towards our desired outcomes.

To master the art of timing for success, it's crucial to develop self-awareness and intuition. Paying attention to our instincts and inner voice can provide valuable insights into when to take action, when to adjust our strategies, and when to seize opportunities. Additionally, learning from past experiences and observing successful individuals in our fields can provide valuable lessons and guidance on how to navigate timing effectively.

Timing is a critical factor in achieving success and reaching our goals. It involves knowing when to start, when to adjust, when to seize opportunities, and when to persevere. By mastering the art of timing, we can enhance our chances of success and set ourselves on the path to realizing our dreams. So, let's embrace the power of timing and use it as a valuable tool in our journey towards success.

VIKKI JONES

DESIGNER

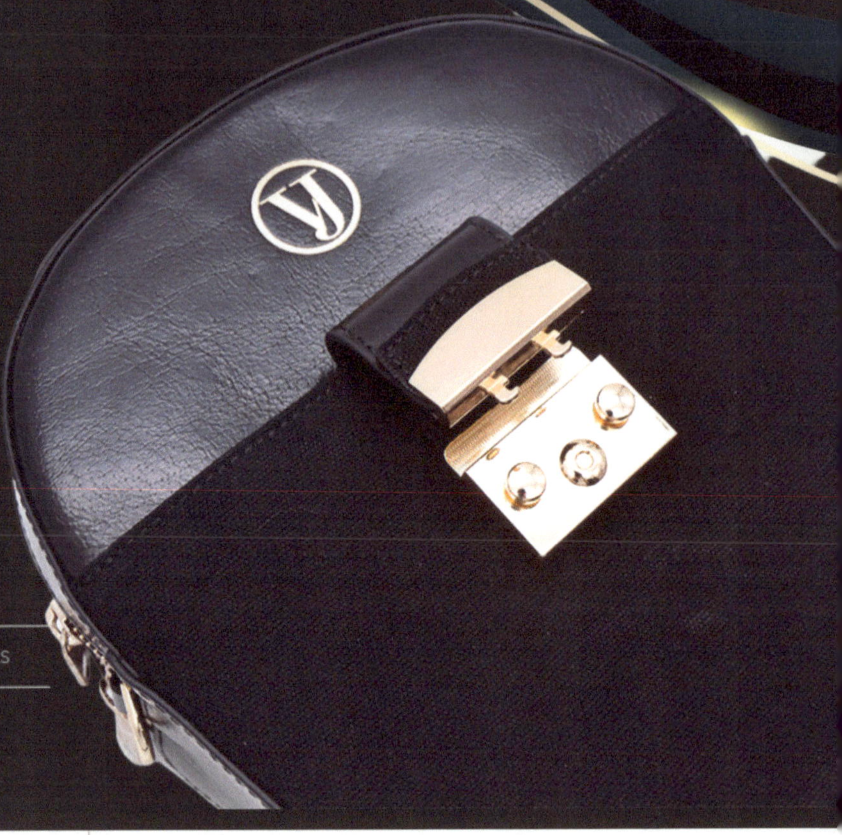

LUXURY LUGGAGE & BAGS | FOR SUCCESSFUL PROFESSIONALS

COMFORTABLE CARRYING OPTIONS

Say goodbye to uncomfortable bags. Vikki Jones' designs prioritize comfort, with padded straps, ergonomic handles, and lightweight construction, ensuring a comfortable carrying experience even during long journeys.

Need extra space? Jones' bags feature expandable compartments, allowing you to increase the capacity when needed. Travel with confidence, knowing you have room for souvenirs or extra work documents.

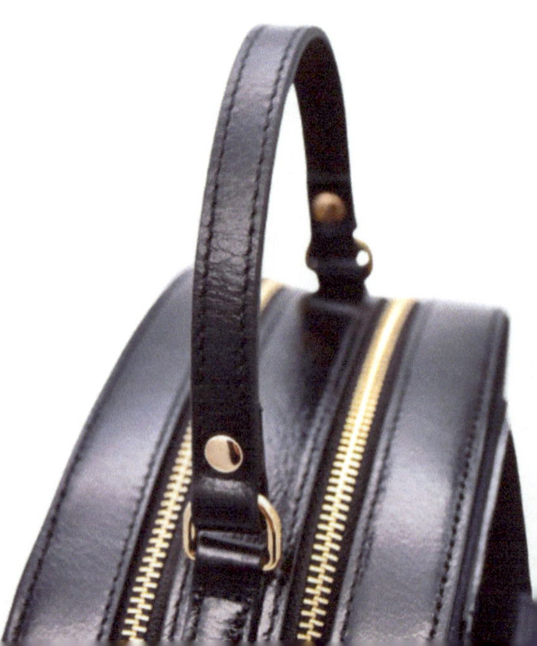

VMH TV CHANNEL ON Roku

VIKKI JONES SHOW
VMH TV

Join host Vikki Jones on VMH TV Channel on ROKU for a talk show that will ignite your passion. Experience thought-provoking discussions with influential guests, heartwarming stories of resilience, and expert insights.

CATCH THE
VIKKI JONES SHOW
ON VMH TV CHANNEL
ON ROKU!

VMH TV CHANNEL

DOWNLOAD APP

NOW STREAMING ON Roku

HOST
VIKKI JONES
VMH MAGAZINE & TV

Mastering the Mindset: Letting Go with Confidence

Written by Vikki Jones

Those who possess a mindset that understands the power of doing what they can and trusting that the rest will fall into place, open doors to a life filled with joy, productivity, and abundance. This transformative mindset allows individuals to advance in less time, realizing that what is meant for them will come their way, and nothing can impede their journey towards greatness.

The key to unlocking this powerful mindset lies in adopting an unwavering belief that each of us holds the capacity to produce our best work, be the best version of ourselves, and continuously strive for personal growth. It is this unwavering commitment to self-improvement that propels individuals towards their goals, enabling them to surpass limitations and achieve remarkable success.

By embracing this positive mindset, we tap into a wellspring of joy that fuels our actions and fuels our productivity. When we approach tasks with a sense of purpose and enthusiasm, we not only enjoy what we do, but we also find that we accomplish more in less time. This is because joy and productivity go hand in hand - when we are genuinely passionate about our work, we become more focused, creative, and efficient. As a result, we are able to achieve our goals faster and with greater ease.

Furthermore, this mindset attracts abundance into our lives. When we align our thoughts and actions with positivity and gratitude, we open ourselves up to a world of limitless possibilities. It is through this mindset that we attract opportunities, connections, and resources that contribute to our personal and professional growth.

However, it is crucial to remember that this mindset does not guarantee a life free from challenges or setbacks. Instead, it equips us with the resilience and determination to overcome obstacles and learn from failures. By focusing on our own growth and development, we become better equipped to navigate through life's inevitable hurdles, emerging stronger and more resilient with each experience.

In conclusion, adopting a mindset that understands the power of doing what we can and trusting that the rest will fall into place is a transformative approach to life. It brings forth joy, productivity, and abundance, allowing us to advance in less time. By acknowledging that what is meant for us will come our way, we can focus on producing our best work, being the best versions of ourselves, and continuously striving for personal growth. So, let us embrace this mindset and unlock our boundless potential, for it is within us to create a life filled with success, fulfillment, and happiness.

JUNIPER GLOBAL

SUPPLY CHAIN SOLUTIONS

OUR SERVICES

- Procurement
- Production
- Supply
- Product Design
- Transportation
- Deliver Finished Product

LEARN MORE

 www.juniperglobalvision.com

THE CHARMS OF ICELAND THROUGH THE LENS OF A SOLO TRAVELER - JERICA COLÓN

Jerica Colón embarked on an awe-inspiring solo adventure to Iceland, driven by her unwavering desire to explore the extraordinary landscapes of this captivating country. In a candid conversation, she revealed the motivation behind her journey, saying, "I was inspired to embark on a solo trip to Iceland because of my long-standing desire to visit the country, yet I lacked any companions. Although I had been yearning to go since 2016, I repeatedly postponed due to a variety of reasons. As time passed, I realized that I was not making any headway in achieving this goal. To my astonishment, my photographs of Iceland garnered great attention and were recently displayed at a photography exposition. The audience was bewitched by the striking landscapes of Iceland."

Traveling solo allows for a unique experience, enabling travelers to immerse themselves fully in the journey's every aspect. Exploring Iceland by tour bus or car, Jerica found herself captivated by the breathtaking views outside her window. She shared, "The rolling hills and majestic mountains all contribute to the scenic beauty that surrounds you. The ever-changing landscape offers a sense of awe and wonder, making each moment of the journey truly special. I believe that it is possible to capture beautiful imagery even from afar or from a car in Iceland, leaving a lasting impression. Hopefully, in the future, I can visit again and explore other parts of the island."

For Jerica, being a photographer means more than just capturing pretty pictures; it entails immersing herself in the essence of each place she visits. To convey the beauty of Iceland through her lens, she prioritizes connecting with locals and gaining insights into their customs, preferences, and local cuisine. She explained, "Understanding the diverse mix of people visiting the same areas allows me to capture authentic moments and interactions in my photographs."

When it comes to the technical aspects of capturing Iceland's grandeur, Jerica emphasized the importance of having a wide-angle lens. This lens enables her to encapsulate the vastness and magnificence of Iceland's landscapes, from towering waterfalls to expansive lava fields. Furthermore, with Iceland's unpredictable weather conditions, a water-resistant camera becomes an indispensable companion. Armed with the right equipment, Jerica fearlessly braves the rain and wind to seize stunning images even in the face of challenging weather conditions.

Jerica's solo journey to Iceland showcases the sheer beauty of this land of fire and ice. Through her lens, she beckons us to appreciate the enchanting allure of Iceland, reminding us that sometimes, venturing forth alone leads to the most extraordinary experiences.

FIRE & ICE

Jerica Colón (Photo Courtesy of Jerica Colón)

"When it comes to the technical aspects of capturing Iceland, having a wide-angle lens is crucial. Iceland's landscapes are vast, awe-inspiring, and feature towering waterfalls and expansive lava fields. This lens allows me to capture the grandeur of these natural wonders. In addition, a water-resistant camera is essential given the unpredictable weather conditions, including rain and wind. Having the right equipment prepares me to capture stunning images even in challenging weather conditions" - Jerica Colón

Follow Jerica Colón @jericacolonphotography

Offering Funding

Accion Opportunity Fund

American Express partnered with Accion Opportunity Fund, a leading non-profit small business lender, on a new program to provide loans and other resources to underfunded small business owners in the U.S., including people of color, women and immigrants. American Express is providing $40M to Accion Opportunity Fund, the largest investment the nonprofit has received since its founding.

Coalition to Back Black Business

American Express established the Coalition to Back Black Businesses, a first-of-its-kind collaboration with the U.S. Chamber of Commerce Foundation and four major Black chambers, including the National Black Chamber of Commerce, the National Business League, the U.S. Black Chambers, Inc., and Walker's Legacy. The Coalition provides grants to Black-owned businesses to support their long-term resilience. The company made a $10 million commitment to fund the grant program and support Black-owned small business recovery in the U.S. over the next four years.

100 for 100

Together with IFundWomen of Color, American Express launched the 100 for 100 program, surprising 100 Black women entrepreneurs with grants of $25,000 each and access to 100 days of business resources – including business education, mentorship, marketing, virtual networking and more – to help them jumpstart their ventures.

Backing Historic Small Restaurants

American Express, in partnership with the National Trust for Historic Preservation, launched "Backing Historic Small Restaurants," a more than $1 million investment to preserve historic restaurants in the U.S. as they continue to navigate the pandemic and plan for recovery. 25 historic and culturally significant restaurants across the U.S. owned by underrepresented groups have received funding and resources.

Providing Tools & Resources

Business Class is a suite of educational and entertaining business resources, in the form of content and events, all available at no cost. American Express has created hundreds of resources for the small business community under the Business Class umbrella, including articles on the Business Trends & Insights website, Daily Edit e-newsletters and "Office Hours" on Instagram Live where followers hear from well-known entrepreneurs.

THE BOOKSHELF

VMH PUBLISHING

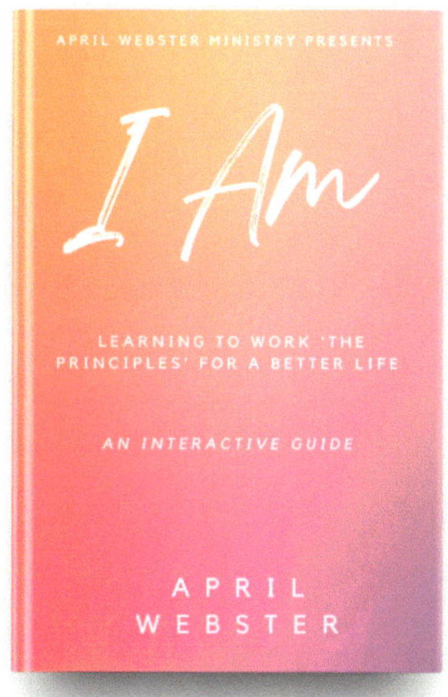

I AM - Learning To Work 'The Principles' For a Better Life

In this book, Dr. April Webster explores twelve affirmations to declare inward strength to her readers. I AM is a metaphysical name of the spiritual self. It is the presence of God with in you. When the words I AM are spoken it is a declaration. I AM is the mere fact of our existence and once you become aware of it you hold the power in your words. Dr. Webster has personally discovered the power of spoken words. This is not a book to be read only once then put away on a book shelf or in a storage bin. This book is intended to be read and repeated over and over until one becomes fully aware of who they really are called to be. This book requires the readers to take action.

By following these principles, you hold the power of transforming your life to another level beyond your current position. Dr. Webster provides the steps needed to act and apply these principles to your life. You will walk and operate in another dimension once you become aware of who you really are.

Bootstrap
Start Where You Are with What You Have

Have a great business idea but no capital? It's possible to build and grow a profitable business without external help or capital. With today's digital technology, a business can be established with little money and succeed. Within this book you will find the framework to start, build and scale a business successfully without tapping into another's bank account. "Bootstrap" serves as an empowering and encouraging tool for aspiring entrepreneurs who may feel discouraged by their lack of resources or access to capital. By demonstrating that success can be achieved through resourcefulness and determination, the book motivates individuals to think creatively, tap into their skills and strengths, and embark on their entrepreneurial journey.

My Best Kept Secret Memoir

"My Best Kept Secret Memoir" is a powerful and inspiring collection of personal stories shared by the author, aimed at empowering women who have endured incidents of abuse. Through her heartfelt narratives, she aims to encourage healing, resilience, and the strength to break free from the shackles of abuse. This memoir is an essential read for anyone seeking to reclaim their lives.

Misdiagnosis: Prostate Cancer Survivor

In his book, Fmr. Lt. Garry L. Jones teaches patients how to prevent delayed or misdiagnosis. After suffering years of recurring infections Jones eventually learned the root cause of his suffering - prostate cancer.

DR. APRIL WEBSTER: EMPOWERING WOMEN AND LEADING THE WAY AS AN HBCU ALUM

I was inspired to attend an HBCU by my father. He encouraged me to attend a college or university that would provide an inclusive community where I could grow and develop as a professional, while being immersed in a rich cultural history.

Dr. April Webster

Dr. April Webster, Founder and CEO of Loving Arms, LLC, A'lashell (lipsticks), and April Webster Ministries, is a distinguished individual with a remarkable educational background. Holding a B.A. in Social Work and a M.A. in Public Administration specializing in Human Resources from Kentucky State University, she further pursued her academic journey by obtaining a Ph.D. in Christian Psychology from the International College of Ministry in 2011.

Inspired by her father's advice, she chose to pursue higher education within an inclusive community that celebrates rich cultural heritage.

"I was inspired to attend an HBCU by my father. He encouraged me to attend a college or university that would provide an inclusive community where I could grow and develop as a professional, while being immersed in a rich cultural history," Dr. Webster shared.

During her time at an HBCU, Dr. Webster experienced personal and professional growth, fueling her passion for empowering others through service, wealth creation, and entrepreneurship. Through A'lashell, she empowers women to embrace their beauty and confidence, while April Webster Ministries provides inspirational messages of hope, faith, and resilience.

The inclusive environment of HBCUs played a pivotal role in shaping Dr. Webster's values and principles. She gained a deep appreciation for diversity, ownership, and the empowerment of women. Driven by her HBCU experience, she remains committed to empowering women through A'lashell and inspiring individuals through April Webster Ministries.

HBCUs offer an educational experience that extends beyond the classroom, celebrating the contributions and achievements of African Americans. Immersed in this environment, Dr. Webster developed a profound appreciation for her identity and the impact she could have on society through service, ownership, wealth creation, entrepreneurship, and empowering women.

The influence of HBCUs continues to shape Dr. Webster's personal and professional life even after graduation. The alumni community provides a strong network of support, fostering success, wealth creation, entrepreneurship, and empowerment of women. It is within this network that Dr. Webster finds the inspiration to share her experiences and insights as an international sought-after speaker.

Dr. April Webster's journey through an HBCU education has been transformative. Guided by her father's wisdom, she chose an inclusive college experience that celebrates rich cultural history. As the Founder and CEO of Loving Arms, LLC, A'lashell (lipsticks), and April Webster Ministries, Dr. Webster is proud to be a product of an HBCU education.

In recognition of her influential work, Dr. Webster was honored as a 2023 Sterling Awards recipient for being one of the top 40 most influential women in West TN. She is also a proud member of Delta Sigma Theta Sorority Inc., Jackson TN Alumnae Chapter.

Her commitment to empowering women, inspiring individuals through April Webster Ministries, and the impact of her HBCU education are evident in her work. Dr. Webster's journey serves as a testament to the transformative power of HBCUs, the importance of embracing diversity, and the potential for personal and professional growth within an inclusive community.

www.ingramcontent.com/pod-product-compliance
Lightning Source LLC
Chambersburg PA
CBHW041639110726
48005CB00002B/652